The Cookie Jar

J. W. METTLE

NEWMAN SPRINGS PUBLISHING
320 Broad Street
Red Bank, NJ 07701

First originally published by Newman Springs Publishing 2021

ISBN 978-1-64801-942-5 (Paperback)
ISBN 978-1-63881-319-4 (Hardcover)
ISBN 978-1-64801-943-2 (Digital)

Printed in the United States of America

To all my family and friends who believe
in dreams and stories coming to life.

I dedicate my first venture in storytelling to
all those who have shaped me, inspired me,
and are the reasons why I am who I am today.
To Grandma Delphine Thornton, my wife Gina,
Mom, Jane, Aunt Gloria, Mark, Uncle Curtis, the
entire Mettle family team, and to all my *friends*,
who are also my *family*. Thank you for being you.

In addition, this goes out to *all people* who
believe in unity, diversity, love, and light.

1

hari goes to his grandma's house every day after school to visit his grandma, auntie, uncle, and cousin Chip.

Khari loves his grandma! She's the nicest lady in the whole world!

Grandma makes Khari and cousin Chip peanut butter and jelly sandwiches for snacks every day and asks them about their day.

"How was your day today? What did you learn in school today?"

Khari says, "Today we learned addition! $1+1 = 2$, $2+1 = 3$, $2+3 = 5$!"

Khari adds, "Today we learned primary colors! Red, yellow, blue, white, and black!"

There is always a cookie jar in grandma's kitchen. It's an amazing magical thing to Khari.

"Only one cookie after snack, boys. Anymore and you'll ruin your dinner," Grandma said with a warm smile.

Khari says, "This is the best cookie I've ever had!"

After snack and homework, Khari and Chip always go outside to play with neighborhood friends.

Khari thinks, *I really want another cookie, they were soooo good! But Grandma said not to...I'll just take one more!*

"Khari and Chip make sure to get in their daily fun activities and exercise with neighborhood friends. Homework, then play time!"

A short while later…as the sun is going down…
Grandma opens the back side door.
"Chip, Khari, dinner time, boys!"

Chip and Khari wash their hands and face and sit down for dinner with the family. Grandma always makes the boys wash hands like this:

1. Wet your hands with warm water (not too hot and not too cold).
2. Lather. Use enough soap to cover your entire hands.
3. Wash. Rub fronts and backs of hands and in between fingers. Hum or sing "Twinkle, Twinkle, Little Star" while washing hands to remind you to scrub for twenty seconds.
4. Rinse hands well under running water.
5. Dry with a clean towel or paper towel. If possible, use your paper towel to turn off the sink.

The family always laughed and joked about the day at dinner time, while eating, and sharing family time. Everyone had to finish their meal before getting up, or being excused from the dinner table.

Khari was in a slight panic, thinking, *Grandma was right! I'm not hungry after eating those two cookies! What do I do now? She'll know I disobeyed her, and I'll get in big trouble! I have to finish my dinner!* Khari knew he *had* to eat his dinner. He scarfed down his food. He knew he could not waste his plate!

Khari, "Oh, wow, my tummy is super full! I have a tummy ache!"

Khari hugged his Grandma.

Khari says, "I love you, Grandma, thanks for dinner. I'll always listen to you!"

Grandma hugged him back. "I love you too. I told you the cookie would ruin your dinner," she said with a warm smile and wink.